TRUE STORIES

FROM CHRISSIE GIBSON'S EARLY LIFE IN ROYAL DEESIDE

After the success of Chrissie Gibson's first book, *MEMORIES OF FINZEAN Schooldays 1925 – 1933*, which was published at the age of 77 years, Chrissie has received many requests for further stories. These reminiscences are mainly of the 1930s when there were few cars on the road. Horses were more common than engines, but not everyone looked after their horses or ponies as well as they should have done.

Chrissie's father was a remarkable man who taught his family to care for and respect all creatures. His own skill and knowledge of horses is still talked about by people fortunate enough to have known him. Like many people born in the 19th century, most of his skill was passed down by word of mouth and honed by observation and experience.

Father feeding his ponies in the 1960s.

SAVING DOBBIN

And other true pony tales
from Royal Deeside in the 1930s

Chrissie Gibson

Braw Publishing

© Chrissie Gibson, 1998

Edited by R.G.Forbes

ISBN 0 9531573 1 8

Distribution: BRAW PUBLISHING
01358 721601

Printed by
Cordfall Ltd.
0141 332 4640

Illustrated by Helen Forbes,
    the author's granddaughter.

These stories are only as accurate as a seventy-eight year old's memory will allow. I hope you enjoy a trip back in time to the 1930s with me and my memories.

Chrissie Gibson

Guest at Finzean School

Contents

Alison Wilson with Murphy

SAVING DOBBIN

THE THIRTY SHILLING PONY

When my father saw the state of the Highland Pony he felt so sorry for the pony that he offered to buy the mare, harness and float for thirty shillings (£1.50). The pony was so ill, due to neglect, ignorance and ill treatment that the owner accepted the offer. Although the harness and cart were in need of repair, considering the prices at the time, the pony cost hardly anything. However, Father still had to get the pony home and risked being fined and the pony shot if the law took its rightful course. Father decided to take the risk as he couldn't bear to see an animal in so much pain. The cart was left behind to be collected next day by one of my brothers using our other pony. My brother Bill drove the car back and Father led the ailing pony home, walking her on the soft verges to cut down the dreadful pain in her hooves.

When I saw the pony I couldn't believe my own eyes at her

condition. She was filthy, skinny, her coat was in a poor condition and she could barely walk. Yet she had walked over ten miles to reach the sanctuary of our stable, as it was the only way Father could get her home. I still feel angry when I think back to that day and realise that the previous owner may have gone on to treat other horses in a similar manner. I made up my mind then that if she recovered she would never suffer needlessly again.

Father was probably very tired himself but he took care of the pony immediately. First he covered her with a thick blanket, to protect her against the cold air of early Spring. The shoes were not only worn through, but were too small when they were fitted. The hooves were badly cracked inflicting severe pain on what we thought at the time was a poor old horse of about twelve or thirteen years of age. Father had his own set of tools for treating our horses feet. He removed the shoe from a foreleg and lowered the hoof into a wooden bucket of warm, slightly salted water. When the pain had eased he tied a soaking sack to the hoof and repeated the treatment with the other hooves. The sacks were like soft slippers after wearing badly fitting shoes and the water helped suck out the dirt from the cracks. Father then let the pony graze for a while, letting it pick its own soft ground.

"She's had enough handling today, she's too weak to put up with any other treatment. Put a thick layer of straw in her stall and give her a good feed of bruised corn Chrissie. I'll have another look at her tomorrow."

Next day Father soaked her feet again and rubbed in oil. I

washed the pony down as she was my responsibility now. Father said that if I cared for her and she recovered then she was mine. First I cropped her mane as it was in such a mess it would have been impossible to comb. Then, as I washed her mane with a very mild solution of Jeye's Fluid, just a drop or two in a bucket of water, I decided to give her an unusual name. I would give her a name that none of the other horses in our area had, as I wanted her to feel special. I thought of a book I had of stories about horses. There was a picture of a proud, carriage horse called Dobbin, which had a cropped mane. I decided to call my pony Dobbin and I was determined that she would make a full recovery.

Poor old Dobbin's coat was so dirty that I couldn't tell what colour she was. Underneath the many layers of dirt, her coat was falling out and bare in patches. It would have been cruel to try and brush her coat, so I continued washing her down with a soft cloth until her coat grew back and fed her oil cake to make her coat shine.

Father looked at her hooves every day and cleaned her hooves with oil which he rubbed into the hard part of the hooves. I was surprised how quickly the hooves healed and grew. After just over a fortnight, Father felt they had recovered enough to be fitted with new shoes, so I took Dobbin to the blacksmith at Strachan about six miles away. The blacksmith at Finzean was nearer, but the road was rougher and there were a lot of gates to open and close behind us. I was able to lead Dobbin almost all the way to Strachan on the soft verge.

The smith was reluctant to shoe Dobbin as there were still deep cracks in her hooves and as most of his customers were farmers bringing him heavy, working horses, his shoes were a bit heavy for a pony. When I told him it was my father's decision to fit her with shoes, he agreed. He fitted larger shoes than she would normally have worn as they were padded with rubber. At that time a set of horses shoes usually cost 18 shillings (90 pence). Dobbin's shoes that day cost me £1-3/ shillings (£1.15). More than Dobbin cost on her own when Father bought her.

Dobbin didn't wear these shoes for long. Her feet were healing quickly despite the heavy shoes, which were only temporary. She needed these shoes to walk the extra distance to the Farrier at Torphins, who shod all the ponies in our area. He also fitted racehorses with lightweight racing shoes. All the smiths were good and gentle with horses and ponies, but Mr. Gall at Torphins built up a special relationship with Dobbin and she learned to trust him. Animals who have been ill-treated need consistency. They need reassurance that they will be cared for. I always took her to Torphins to be shod and stood at her head holding the bridle while Mr. Gall talked softly and kindly to Dobbin throughout her visit.

The shoes were made to fit Dobbin's hooves. Now that he had measured her hooves, he made up a spare set of shoes when he wasn't busy as he did for all the ponies and horses. The shoes hung on the wall in sets, with the name of each pony. A set of shoes would last about three or four months. We never let our ponies' shoes wear right through, or had them fitted with old shoes which could have a bar added to make them last longer. One thing that did puzzle me was the way the shoes seemed to wear out more quickly when Dobbin spent most of her time on soft ground.

The speed at which Dobbin recovered amazed us, even when we realised that she was younger than we first thought. Her mane grew back thick and long. Her coat grew in and she regained the weight she had lost. In fact she looked as if she was getting younger every day. She was a handsome pony, taller than average with a muscular neck and sturdy body which is a sign of a true Highland pony or garron. She was brown with a black mane and a black stripe along her back. Dobbin was only about two or three years old and was not properly broken in. The harness and float, a flat cart with two wheels, had been repaired and soon it was time to try her out with them.

Dobbin was reluctant to go in the shafts at first and I had to finish the job of breaking her in. She loved snacks of carrots and oil cake, or an extra feed of oats or corn, so it was easy to train her with kindness. She willingly pulled her light float, which was never overloaded. Getting her to pull the lighter gig was a different matter. I felt that either the quieter rubber wheels unnerved her as she could hardly tell where the gig was, or she had a bad experience with a gig before Father bought her. Dobbin didn't actually refuse, she was just so jittery that it didn't seem worthwhile forcing her into it when she willingly pulled the float.

Dobbin never got over her fear of men. Even my father's voice made her start. If any man spoke to her when she was harnessed to the cart, perhaps waiting outside a shop, she would kick out sideways as a warning, or bare her teeth and whinny. Yet she loved children and would go to them to be petted and was always playful with me and my younger brothers and sisters. Dobbin would whinny for attention and if I pretended not to notice her she would come up to me from behind and push me with her nose. She would do this several times then make a sound which was a cross between neighing and chuckling. Father said she was more in character like a dog than a horse and would sniff the air for my scent. If I went out in the car I always told her that I was going out. I stroked her face and told her she had the day off, reassuring her that I would be back later to put her in her stall. When I returned she would meet the car and show she was pleased to see me. Dobbin was more like a friend, a member of our family, than a possession or beast of burden.

I came to the conclusion that Dobbin's previous owner kept her outside in all weather. She seemed to have a fear of being left out, even in warm summer weather. When she was ready to go to her stall she didn't wait for me to put her in. She would come to the living room window and whinny for me, then go to the stable door. Sometimes in mild weather Dobbin would want to go to her stall early. At first I thought she felt ill and worried that she would be sick next day, but as she always seemed to be fit the following morning I assumed she just needed a little extra reassurance.

I used to get out the scythe and cut fresh green grass and other plants she enjoyed eating and put this in her stall. When she was in her stall Dobbin liked to eat while lying on her side, then she would go to sleep in the same position. I would go back later and cover her with a blanket. She was always sleeping soundly and snoring loudly. I was afraid she wouldn't get enough to eat if she kept going to her stall early. I also wanted her to know that I cared so that she would stop worrying. I suppose nowadays people would say she was depressed. When a horse is so nervous that it is startled when you pat it and seems to be afraid that you will strike it, then it needs a lot of love and attention to overcome its fears.

Eventually Dobbin was so well trained that she would do anything I asked, but it took time. When I first took Dobbin with me to shop in Banchory, I took one of my brothers or sisters with me. At one time there were rings to tether horses to, outside of the shops in the High Street. These had been removed, but I was still responsible for Dobbin and by law a horse should not be left on its own. I would stay with Dobbin while my brother or sister went into the shop with our order and the grocer brought it out to the float. Later on, when my brothers and sisters were in school, I tied the reins to the shaft to keep her head still, if the grocer was too busy to come out and ask for our order.

Gradually I trusted her enough to stand still without a tight rein, but only if there were no other horses nearby and no steam engines within earshot. The steam engines were very loud and Dobbin used to get so upset that I was afraid she would bolt, as there were no brakes on two wheeled gigs or carts in those days. I knew Dobbin would stand still for me while I went into the grocer's shop when they were busy. Usually I was only there for a minute or two; just long enough to give them my order, which would be made up in the shop and carried out to the cart where I paid for it.

One day I saw Flo, an old school friend, when I went into the shop with the order. I wanted to speak to Flo as she had moved to Banchory and I hadn't seen her for some time. While I was there I could keep an eye on Dobbin, but she also caught the attention of the local Bobby. Banchory was busier that day than it usually was on a weekday and Dobbin was looking about, giving the impression that she was restless. I knew the constable quite well and usually he was a friendly helpful man. That day he had the idea that Dobbin might run off. He knew she had been ill treated in the past and had been a nervous horse, so I don't blame him for thinking that she wasn't under control. As I was only about sixteen years old he probably thought I lacked experience with horses. I carried my groceries out to the float and said hallo. He told me I was breaking the law, not having someone in charge of the horse. Considering the big horse drawn delivery vans had to be left unattended when the drivers made their deliveries I felt he was being a bit unfair.

"If you think you can move my horse you are welcome to try." I could see Dobbin was listening and understood every word I said to the Bobby. "My pony knows not to move, she's a good girl." I patted her neck as I said this and she understood. He took me at my word and tried to command Dobbin to move. She stood perfectly still, ignoring him. Then he tried other commands, but still Dobbin ignored the policeman. Finally he tried leading her away, without success.

"You must have been very cruel to Dobbin to get her to stand as still as that." By now a crowd was gathering and he was beginning to look rather silly.

"Not at all. I wouldn't ill treat any animal, but I'll show you how to move Dobbin." The Bobby expected me to give a secret command or sign, as I drove off. Instead, standing well back and using a normal voice I said "Come on Dobbin, we'll go to the bakers' next". Off Dobbin walked, stopping in front of the bakers' shop. She then looked round at the bobby and neighed. The Grocer said "I think she's laughing at you constable."

I stroked Dobbin's neck and praised her for being a good girl, while I rewarded her with a piece of oil cake. I think I proved to anyone that day that I had perfect control of Dobbin, providing there were no heavy steam engines about.

When I was out with Dobbin people would call out to me, telling me how good our pony looked. I was very proud of her and once her coat grew in I brushed her every day until her coat shone. Her mane grew in thick and long. Sometimes she seemed to take a delight in tossing her long mane, as if she was also proud of her appearance. I spoke to her as if she was another human being and was surprised by how much she seemed to understand. Sharing my teenage years with Dobbin was a wonderful experience, like having one's dearest wish come true, without having to ask for it. However, all good things come to an end and soon it would become necessary to part with Dobbin for ever.

I had been released from Finzean School almost a year early, when I was only thirteen. I was given an exemption certificate as my mother needed me at home, she was run down after having several children in her forties. Now that my two youngest brothers were at school and my other younger brothers and sisters were more able to look after one another, there was less to do. Mother seemed to need less rest now, but the real change came when a stranger called at our house one day accompanied by one of our neighbours.

Mr. Fraser introduced a man from the government, who was calling on all the households in our area. It had seemed likely for some time that a war with Germany was looming. We were given identity cards, gas masks, asked for our dates of birth and whether we all had jobs. He was drawing up a register of volunteers who could be called upon at short notice if war was declared. My parents thought it would be a good idea if I added my name to the list. They assumed that I would join the land army as many young women from the country had done in the first world war; this was probably in 1938, when I was eighteen years old. As time went on and war seemed more and more likely, I felt it would be a good idea to find Dobbin a good home while I still had time to arrange this myself. I was also rather worried that I would be sent to a noisy, confining factory to do war work, so I decided to take matters into my own hands and find work on the land.

I told Father that I wanted to find a good home for Dobbin before I was forced to leave home at short notice. Of all the people who admired and petted Dobbin, one lassie came to mind. I can still remember her expression when she first saw Dobbin, the loving way she spoke to Dobbin and said she wished Dobbin was her horse. She was probably only a year or two younger than I was and Dobbin seemed to take a particular liking to the lassie. I remember the lassie as if it were yesterday and yet I can't remember her Christian name. Although I'm seventy-eight years old now and didn't see this lassie very often, I liked her and trusted her to care for Dobbin; so I find this lapse of memory very disappointing. I think the family's name was Grant. Her father owned a farm near Aboyne and seemed to treat his work-horses well. A few days later Father told me to take Dobbin along to their farm as the farmer was interested in buying Dobbin and was also willing to buy the harness and the float.

It was with a heavy heart that I drove Dobbin for the last time. Dobbin shared my life for about three or four years, which was a very happy time for me. It was now my responsibility to make the hand over as easy as possible for Dobbin and the new owners, but first I wanted to make sure that Mr. Grant was willing to keep Dobbin until the end of her days. Mr. Grant was a very kind man and promised me that if he ever had to part with Dobbin he would sell her back to us.

I remember asking £10 for Dobbin, the harness and the float. Mr. Grant paid me without haggling. I advised them to get Dobbin shod at the farrier at Torphins as Mr. Gall always had a set of shoes ready for her. Dobbin wouldn't need to be shod for a while, which would give her time to get used to her new mistress. Before I left I watched the lassie unharness Dobbin and practise harnessing and hitching Dobbin, so that Dobbin would understand this was her new owner. I also told them that Dobbin was particularly fond of oil cake and carrots. I had to be sure that they knew how to look after Dobbin and were aware of all her likes and dislikes as I could never bring myself to go back there. Dobbin belonged to them now, but I knew if I saw her again that I would want to take her back and she might want to come with me; although I was invited to visit her at any time it would have been too painful an experience.

My father was waiting for me at the end of their farm road so I had to walk past the field where they had put Dobbin. Dobbin ran alongside of me, on the other side of the fence, whinnying. I stroked her face for the last time and told her she had to be good with her new owner. I also assured her that she was going to be happy there and would be well looked after. I can't describe the way I felt when father drove me away, but I think it must be similar to the way I would feel if ever I had been forced to leave one of my children for good. After that day I only saw Dobbin from a distance.

Sometimes I passed Dobbin in the car while she was out with her new owner. She looked well cared for. When I took a pony to the Torphins' Farrier, I asked if Dobbin was still being shod there. Mr. Gall pointed to her shoes on the wall and assured me that they told him to keep a spare set of shoes for her. I was glad

I had made the right choice when I sold Dobbin to Mr. Grant.

Several years after Dobbin was sold, my father saw Dobbin with her new mistress, while they were shopping in Aboyne. He wouldn't have approached Dobbin as she was always easily startled by men, but the lassie spoke first as she was eager to tell him how happy she was with Dobbin. On hearing Father's voice, Dobbin neighed for attention. Father spoke kindly to her for a minute or two. When he walked away poor Dobbin started neighing repeatedly, in a manner that she always used when she was upset or felt threatened; she sounded as if she was calling for help or attention. Father drove away hearing the mournful sound for some distance. He said I was right not going back to visit my old friend.

In time Dobbin's new owner also left home, but Dobbin had learned to trust Mr. Grant. She even adapted to pulling the gig. After the float became a strain to pull, the much lighter gig was the ideal vehicle. Mr. Grant would never overwork a horse or pony.

When the time came for Mr. Grant to retire from his farm, my father offered to buy Dobbin back as he feared she would eventually end up with a less understanding owner. He needn't have worried. Mr. Grant retired to a small croft with a stable. He took Dobbin with him and had a field where she would spend her last days. He also sent me a message that I could have the horse back, as a gift. I don't know if he was afraid that Dobbin would outlive him, but as I lived in a flat in Aberdeen at the time, taking Dobbin back was out of the question.

Over twenty years after my father rescued Dobbin, my husband started taking our children to visit Dobbin, now and again, to feed her carrots. Then he found work in England and we were forced to leave Aberdeen for a while. The year was now 1956. I sat in our car and watched my old friend, who was now turning grey in places, as she walked slowly to the fence with her ears twitching and tail swishing to show how happy she was to see them. It was a very sad moment for me, but it shouldn't have been. She must have been about twenty-five years old at the time, a great age for a horse to reach. For over twenty years she's been shown only kindness. I knew she would live out her life here and when her heart eventually gave out she would be laid to rest at the back of the house; where children who loved her could visit her grave.

Now that I'm old, lame and blind, I sometimes think back to happier times. I can still feel Dobbin's soft fur as I stroke her face. I can remember her grunt, similar to a chuckle and see her ears twitch every few seconds listening in different directions as Highland Ponies have a tendency to do. Sometimes I drop off to sleep in my armchair and wake suddenly imagining that I'm sitting on the float. For a second or two I think I can see Dobbin, tail swishing, coat gleaming and head held high as she clip clops along the road. Like Dobbin in her later years I've a lot of happy memories to be thankful for.

NELLIE

Father bought Nellie while I still owned Dobbin. Nellie was a young garron, about one and a half to two years old and only partly broken in. She was a tall pony, about the same height as Dobbin but lighter in weight and all black. Her soft black velvety coat shone and father also bought her gig, which was well designed and made. Together they were strikingly beautiful, a pony and gig which anyone would be proud to own. I couldn't understand at the time why the previous owner sold them; particularly as Nellie was a very intelligent pony and the easiest trained pony I ever saw.

Father loved driving Nellie with her gig. She needed experience before being sold on to someone who might lack skill driving horses or ponies. When father left Nellie at home my younger brothers and sisters played with her as she was docile, playful and loved being with children. Mother didn't pay a lot of attention to what the younger ones were doing, as Andy and Jimmy should have been old enough to know how to look after horses and ponies. She just told me to check up on what they were doing, from time to time. When I did check on their games I could hardly believe what they were up to.

Jimmy and Andy were fascinated by circus horses and wanted Nellie to do the same tricks. Jimmy, who was four years younger than me at the time acted as trainer and ringmaster. He just had to say "Look Nellie, bow down like this, or walk like this. Walk on three legs like this Nellie." and she did it. They had her turning round on the spot and walking sideways, like a dressage horse. Then Jimmy told her to stand on her two hind legs, then walk about on two legs. The more practice she had walking on two legs, the further she was able to walk. I have to admit that I was very impressed by their act at first.

Bare back riding was common already, with my brothers and sisters, but I was alarmed to find them attempting trick riding while Nellie rode round in circles. I felt it was time to intervene. "No jumping on or off a moving pony as you could get trampled by accident." After this I seemed to be always stopping them from going too far, but I didn't want to complain to my parents all the time; even when they tried something very silly.

Nellie was willing to try anything Jimmy asked and was about to try jumping through a hoop when I stopped the trick. I pointed out to my bams of brothers that the gird they were using was too small. If she did manage to jump into it without tripping, the gird would get stuck on her body. "How would they explain that to Ma?" As I had sold Dobbin by now, I had more time to check up on what they were doing. I heard loud banging from a tea chest and investigated their latest trick. Nellie was standing on her hind legs again, but this time her forelegs were thumping an upturned tea chest.

"Down Nellie, and don't try that trick again. Jimmy, don't ask Nellie to do that trick as she could get hurt. Andy, you're older. You should have stopped him. If I find out you're trying that again, I'll see to it that Nellie gets sold, very quickly!" A

few days later I heard louder thumping from the tea chest, accompanied by a loud drum roll. I rushed outside, then called for my mother. "Come outside, quick Ma come outside and see what the younger one's are daeing."

Nellie was standing on the tea chest, with all four hooves on the chest. She seemed to be proudly showing off to an audience of my younger brothers and sisters, nieces and nephews and neighbours' children. Ma ordered Nellie off the tea chest and told her off. Then she turned to Jimmy. "If the tea chest

28

splits you'll break poor Nellie's legs and she'll have to be put doon. How happy will you feel then? I'm going to tell your father to sell Nellie before she has an accident, or one of the younger bairns are injured." The tea chest was sawn up that day. It was obvious that the pony would have to be sold as Jimmy lacked common sense. Sooner or later he would try some other dangerous trick and he might be less lucky next time.

A few days later, after surviving her circus acts unharmed, Nellie almost died in a freak road accident. Father was driving the gig with Nellie. Bill, one of my older, sensible brothers, was in the passenger seat. They were travelling along a narrow, country road when suddenly Father was dazzled by bright sunlight reflected off a car's mirror or chrome parts, temporarily blinding him. In that same instant Nellie leapt off the road to the left verge, which was really a deep ditch. The left shaft broke, Bill received bruises and shock and Nellie strained her back and was also badly bruised. Father was unhurt, but badly shocked. He thought Bill was dead and Nellie would have to be put down. Both recovered, but it took months of careful nursing before Nellie recovered.

Nellie never seemed the same again. The mischievous spark in her personality had gone. Father repaired the gig and re-trained Nellie, calming her down more than before. She was sold to an elderly couple, who father knew would be kind to her. He didn't want her working hard as he wasn't completely sure that she had fully recovered from the accident. There might have been a deep injury that wasn't obvious to him at the time.

She seemed happy with her new owners who had her for quite a few years.

Sometimes we stopped the car beside her field and she would trot over to the dyke to greet us. We would chat away to Nellie and stroke her rich velvety coat once more. Although she never forgot us I wonder if she had fond memories of her time as an amateur circus show pony. Did she remember Jimmy and Andy as the trainer and ringmaster? I'm sure Margaret, Elsie and my niece Mary had a great time playing circus riders while Geordie, Robbie and others were the audience.

OTHER PONIES

Father bought many ponies over the years. They were usually Highland ponies, either the smaller Western Isles ponies, the mainland garrons or cross bred garrons. His favourite ponies were garrons crossed with Norwegian ponies. These ponies were known locally as Glen Tanar ponies, as they were introduced to the area by the Glen Tanar Estate, after the second laird married a Norwegian lady. They were unusual looking ponies, light in colour with black manes, black tails and a black dorsal stripe along their backs. They were strong, hard working horses with gentle natures.

Most Highland ponies are sturdy, easy to manage and require little medical attention. Father could usually tell a good horse at horse fairs, with little more than a glance. However, some problems are impossible to see even with close examination.

Father bought a pony at a horse fair, which seemed to be a good buy. It was a healthy looking young mare with a shiny coat. She was also very placid natured and was easy to train. Getting her to chew her food was a different matter. I remember watching our new pony in amazement, as she pulled out the grass in tufts, sucked it, then discarded it. When I told Father he watched her and said he'd heard about horses who couldn't chew due to improperly formed teeth. Some people said they had hollow teeth. We were not going to pull them out to find out what the problem was. Father chopped up grass for her, which she managed to swallow. While he was doing this our new pony was so hungry she rode in among the hens and ducks to steal their

food. She was particularly fond of boiled tatties. One of my brother's named her Duke's Nose. It took time and patience to find a way of feeding her regularly without turning this into a full time job.

Duke's Nose could eat soft food such as mashed raw turnips and potatoes; oil cake, if cut up small enough and well bruised corn. As long as the food was soft she would raise her head and shake her head about until the food just slipped down. She could swallow, but she couldn't move her food to the back of her mouth first. Duke's Nose was sold to someone who was looking for a gentle natured horse to pull a gig. Father was completely honest about her eating problem and told the new owner before closing the deal, how to feed her. The new owner was quite happy with his pony and no doubt changed her name. He had time to care for her properly and I should imagine got her at a bargain price. It was worthwhile telling people about the animals they were buying as Father was sometimes asked for a pony by someone who didn't want an excitable horse, or were inexperienced drivers. They knew they could trust Father to be honest.

Another pony which had an eating problem, had no trouble with its teeth; it just had a habit of eating wood. Fortunately Father found out about this habit before putting it in its stall for the night, or it would have been pretty ill by morning. We used to joke about having a pony who would eat its way out of its home, or through a wooden gate. We didn't have it very long, although it wasn't a problem. Father just covered the top edge of the stall with metal, which didn't interest her. She was sold to a man who was warned not to let her near wooden posts, or gates and to protect her stall. She always found bits of wood to chew but it didn't seem to do her any harm.

The gentle nature of garrons, made them a favourite pony with many people. Queen Victoria's love of these Highland ponies made them very popular during her later years. In recent years they have become an ideal horse for disabled riders. They are a very intelligent breed and I wouldn't be a bit surprised if they are the most intelligent of the British mountain and moorland pony breeds.

Pure bred Highland ponies are becoming rare, as cross breeding with other breeds, mainly Arabian horses, are producing taller, lighter ponies which are already more common than the true garron.

THE HIGH STEPPING HORSE

Occasionally Father would bring home a horse instead of a pony. The strangest horse he ever bought must have been Polly, a fine looking chestnut mare, with the look of a thoroughbred. She was a tall horse and very proud. Father called her a high stepper. She also held her head and tail high and I felt as if she was saying "Look at me. I am a fine horse, better than all the others."

Father tried her out with the gig. She was useless at pulling the gig as her steps became even higher and she was far too slow. She only seemed to have one speed, which was equal to a slow walking pace, and she would not be hurried. Worse was to follow. When father pulled her up she went into fancy side-stepping movements, like a dressage display. This can be a bit worrying when your horse looks as if it's going to dance into a parked vehicle, or mount the pavement. Father was relieved when he finally came to the end of their first little trip, then Polly went into a low graceful bow which suddenly lowered the front of the two wheeled gig. I was glad that I didn't have to go out on the road with Polly, but Father always tried out our horses and ponies first and he set about the task of re-training Polly right away.

It was very easy to train Polly to do something new, but she seemed incapable of unlearning, or adjusting what she had already learned and would never have been able to work alongside another horse. When she was saddled, she just wanted to go into a whole dressage routine. Father came up with a brilliant solution. He sold Polly to a circus.

He told the circus owner that she would be hopeless with his troupe of horses and would only work on her own. When the circus boss saw Polly go through her high stepping routine, like Father, he could see Polly's potential and Father received a very good price for her.

When the circus came back to our area a year later, Father was sitting in the audience in the hope of seeing Polly. Proudly Polly led all the other acts out. She looked as if she was thoroughly enjoying herself and when she bowed down to the audience a great cheer went up. Children in particular adored her. Polly had also been taught new tricks, but the crowd's favourite tricks seemed to be the side stepping and bowing which we were unable to stop her doing.

Polly was a popular act with that circus for many years to come and I think Father must have been very proud of his former horse, as he watched her go through her circus act on that first visit and later seeing her on circus posters and hearing about the fine, high-stepping horse from visitors to the circus.

THE
FARMER'S HORSE

Father's ability with horses was so well known that he probably wasn't surprised when a farmer flagged him down when father was driving past the farm in his old model T Ford. It was easy for the farmer to recognise the car as there were few cars on the road at that time.

"Will you come and look at my horse Davie? The vet's aboot tae shoot it and you're my last hope. It's a young horse and seemed healthy, but it just stopped eating an' drinking."

The farmer walked his horse round the yard. It was skinny and weak. Father could see why the vet insisted the horse should be destroyed. It looked as if it could only live for a few days and was already suffering. The horse had been a willing worker and the farmer was genuinely fond of it. He was a soft hearted man who cared about his animals. It was also expensive to replace a large workhorse and this young farmer had a family depending on him. "The vet looked doon its throat, but there didn't seem to be a blockage. He couldn't find anything else wrong wae my horse."

Father watched the odd way the horse pushed its head forward, stretching its neck and looking as if it was trying to bring something up. Many years before he'd seen an army horse doing the same movement so he had a good idea of what was troubling the horse.

"Hold its heid while I look doon its throat." Father thought he could see where the trouble was coming from. He could see where the lining of the horse's throat was inflamed. He put his hand into the horses mouth. He could feel a wire, which the naked eye couldn't see. Then he went to the toolbox in his car and brought back an ordinary pair of pliers.

For many years after that day, the farmer told the story of how he held the horses head still while Davie reached into the horses mouth and in seconds brought out a piece of wire. The springy, curved wire was very messy after having been embedded in the horses throat for days.

The horse reacted by struggling free with such force that the farmer thought it would attack Father, due to the sudden, severe pain. Instead the horse rubbed its head against Father's face with gratitude. The farmer said that his large workhorse "Looked as if it would have kissed Davie, if it could."

The horse's manner and bearing changed immediately as it knew it was going to recover. Father had told the farmer to have a bucket of tepid water ready to soothe the horses mouth and throat. Despite the pain the horse almost emptied the large bucket of water and then it had a feed of soft mashed corn or oats. When father called in to see the horse, a few days later, the change was remarkable in what had been a dying horse. Most of the lost weight was regained and the horse almost danced over to Father.

Father didn't call in at that farm very often, but when he did, even years after the event the horse wanted to go to him and thank him. Even when it was working in the fields it picked up his scent and let the farmer or his ploughman know it wanted back to the farmyard. They always knew why it wanted back and let it greet Father. The horse seemed to appreciate what father had done for it, until the end of its days.

When I think of the size of the work-horse towering over

my little father, who was only about 5ft. 8in. tall, I should be amazed at his confidence and courage, but I'm afraid I took this for granted. Although I respected and loved my father when I was young, I didn't realise just how lucky I was that my father was such a caring and talented man. In writing these stories of my own experiences with horses, I have come to realise that without really thinking about my reasons for having them printed; they have turned out to be a tribute to my father, instead of just reminiscences of my teenage years.

PEGGY

This book was already finished when Margaret, my youngest daughter, asked me if I had mentioned Peggy. Peggy was my father's favourite pony during his old age and was an exceptional mare who seemed to have a sense of humour which would have been a credit to a human being.

It was during the 1960s, when Father was over eighty years old, that he bought a fine looking, cream coloured garron. Peggy was intelligent and seemed to understand everything Father said to her. He would often be seen feeding Peggy carrots, which seemed to be her favourite tit bits. If anyone crossed her field without offering her a little snack, she would nibble their arm or push them with her nose. She would also whinny a warning when strangers approached.

My nephew Robin was a regular visitor to my parents. His main interest in life, like many boys of his age, was climbing on everything that didn't move out of his way first. His favourite climbing places were the fences and dykes round the ponies' field and he paid no attention to requests or orders to stay off.

"Come doon aff that dyke Robin! You'll knock doon boulders which will injure the ponies." A short while later Father was telling him off again. "Stay aff the fence, I've just repaired the bit you broke earlier. Sharp, rough bits o' wood can hurt the ponies."

Robin argued with his grandfather until he was told "I'll be having a word wae your father this time. I'm not going to let you injure my ponies."

Peggy was listening to this and when Father walked away Robin climbed back on the fence saying "You won't keep me off the fence." She retaliated by head butting Robin's back, knocking him off the fence. Father turned back and asked Robin, who was stretched out on the ground crying and kicking with rage, "What are you screaming at?"

Peggy was standing beside the fence, nodding her head as if she was agreeing with Robin when he complained that she had pushed him off the fence. He got no sympathy from my father. "It's what you deserve for climbing on the fence, you've been told often to stay aff the fence."

When Peggy heard this she galloped about the field as if she was dancing and kicked back her hind legs to show how happy she was. Robin couldn't walk through the field after that incident as Peggy would gallop up to him and whinny. Robin claimed that Peggy was making threatening faces at him.

Shortly after Robin was pushed off the fence, he took an interest in ponies which has stayed with him ever since. He seems to love caring for them as much as my late father did. Some day people may speak about Robin with the same air of awe that I have heard used in reference to my late father.

DOBBIN

Hooves split, an agony of limping.
Neglect by uncaring, cruel hands.
Soft verge, mile upon mile of forcing,
till exhausted, in safety it stands.
Broken hearted, Highland pony.

Cruel shoe off, hoof soaked lovingly.
Warm blanket, kind words, watered and fed.
wash down, hooves oiled, stroked caringly.
Stabled nightly, safely, soft straw bed.
My own Highland pony.

Recovering, shoes nailed skilfully.
Mane growing, coat gleaming, thickening.
Younger, fitter, neighing joyfully.
Proud, head high, tail swishing, galloping.
My happy Highland pony.

Ruby. (Author's daughter.)

The Ponies' Photographs

I would like to thank everyone who answered a national appeal for photographs of Highland ponies. I have used the photographs of ponies which looked most like Dobbin. Unfortunately, none of these were of mares. Dobbin was quite a large and sturdily built mare. Like the geldings in these photographs, Dobbin changed colour with the seasons from a pale beige to a mid brown and some years even dark brown.

Ardle (the front cover picture) is owned by Jennifer Herd of Muirhead, Angus. Murphy (the pictures on pages 9 and 21) is owned by Alison Wilson of Stranraer.

Meeting youngest fan Lindsey Gordon, booksigning at Waterstones Aberdeen.

Chrissie Gibson, the author, would like to add her thanks and also thank all her readers who encouraged her to relate these stories to me. Chrissie hopes you enjoy sharing her experiences with the ponies and horses she grew up with. The next book is already half completed and will probably be called *Auld Bill's Granddaughter.* Auld bill was a gifted storyteller. He was a master of an art which has almost died out in the English speaking world. Chrissie owes much of her skill to Auld Bill and other members of her family who kept this gift alive.

I hope all readers of this book enjoy reading these stories as much as I have enjoyed recording them.

Ruby (Author's daughter)